MANAGING MONEY

PETER MARMARA-STEWART

MANAGING
MONEY

BE A BOSS, TAKE CONTROL
AND LIVE YOUR BEST LIFE

Thank you to my wife Kat, for constantly pushing me and inspiring me to always be my best.

First published in 2022 by PCR Investment Nominees 2 Pty Ltd

A catalogue entry for this book is available from the National Library of Australia.

ISBN: 978-1-922764-21-8

Project management and text design by Publish Central
Cover design by Pipeline Design

CONTENTS

INTRODUCTION

My goal in writing this book is to help more people take ownership of their money, and give them the tools and knowledge to get started on the path to control their financial future. If you're someone who feels you are making good money but never get ahead, this book is for you. You'll learn everything you need to take control and be a boss – with money and in life.

Who am I?

I'm Peter Marmara-Stewart. I run and own an accounting and financial planning business in regional Victoria that serves clients all over Australia.

I started in the financial services industry at the age of 17, and at the time of writing of this book I have been in the industry for 17 years. I started providing financial advice at the age of 19 and took over the accounting business I now run at the age of 23.

I have three children, two of whom are step-children. They are aged 18, 14 and 10. My wife and I have been married for 10 years.

I love my work and how much I can help people achieve their goals. At the age of 34, I am almost in a position where I do not need to work as a result of my financial choices in life. By writing this book, I hope I can help more people take control of their money and lives in the way I have.

So, what should you expect from this book?

This book is designed as a guide and provides you with real action points that you can take, giving you control of your money and financial future. I start by challenging some common mindsets about money that might be holding you back, and will then teach you some of the basics of how to look at money. Some of the insights I'll give you go against conventional wisdom. This book is designed to challenge what most people will tell you so that you can make better choices and own your 'business'. When I say 'business' in this sense, I mean everything that we as adults need to manage in our lives – including managing money.

According to MLC's *Wealth Submission Retirement Income Review*, 55% of Australians who have not yet retired do not think they will have enough money in retirment. Government assistance isn't enough to live off. If you read this book, I guarantee that you will have the information and power you need to take control of your 'business', ensuring you do not fall into that 55%. Not only that, but you will learn some simple hacks that will allow you to live a better life without breaking the bank.

CHAPTER 1

A BOSS MONEY MINDSET

Without the right money mindset, *nothing* you will do will help you get to where you want to go. Why? If you have the wrong mindset, you will self-sabotage. You might not consciously do it but subconsciously you will sabotage your own success. Stupid brain, right?

That is why I talk about money mindset first. If you don't turn around your poor mindset, the rest of this book and anything else you read will be a waste of time. If your goal is to be a boss with money you must spend time resetting your mindset first.

MONEY MYTHS

Let's start with busting some of the myths and socially accepted 'wisdom' around money that could be holding you back. These are some of the things that you (and/or your parents) might believe and say:

- Money doesn't grow on trees.
  - *Actually, if you have paper currency it does. Also, you can make money grow!*

- Money is limited.
  - *There is no limit to the amount of money that the world can produce. You just need to get your slice of the pie!*

- Money is evil.
  - *Money is neither evil nor good. It is nothing more than an exchange of value. The truth is that money is useless and worthless if you have nothing to exchange it for. Imagine being stuck on a desert island with $1 million cash. It won't help you.*

- I am not made of money.
  - *No, but you have unlimited potential to make it! You just need to open your mind to the possibilities.*
- You need to go to uni and get a job to make real money.
  - *Some of the wealthiest people I know didn't even finish high school and some never even had a real job! What you need to do is add value. When you add value people will reward you with money.*
- You need to save for what you want.
  - *Don't save – invest to build cashflow. Cashflow is king!*

Now, let's take a look at some of these myths in more detail.

Money doesn't grow on trees

What is greater – $1 million, or 1 cent that doubles every day for 30 days?

If you said $1 million you would be wrong! 1 cent that doubles every day for 30 days turns into approximately $5.3 million. Now, I am not promising that you can actually do this, but what this example shows is the power of compound interest. Compound interest is the most beautiful thing in the world if you get it working for you. On the other hand, if you have it working against you with high-interest credit cards and other debt it will cause you serious trouble. Compound interest is how you make money grow – it's nothing more than simply putting money away and investing it to get growth and income returns.

Money is limited - I am not made of money

Whatever you want to achieve, you can – you just need to make your goal to get there. There isn't any limit to the amount of money in the world. Money supply is driven by the banks and government and they can issue unlimited amounts of it! All you need to do is start playing their game so that you can get your fair share of the pie.

Money is evil

Money in itself isn't evil or good – it just is. You can either do good things or bad things with money – that is really up to you. If you make millions of dollars you can put that money towards things such as gambling or useless material possessions. Or you can provide funding to your family and chosen charities. Who gives more – the person who makes $1,000 and gives $500, or the person who makes $100,000 and gives $10,000? The answer is the person who gives $10,000. Money can cure a lot of ills and allows you to give more to the causes that you want to support, as well as providing financial security for your family.

You need to go to uni and get a job to make real money

This is probably the most limiting thing that people can tell each other. Let me say that there is nothing wrong with getting a trade or going to university and getting a job to make money. But I think it's wrong when people say doing so is the *only* way to make real money. That couldn't be further from the truth.

I personally believe that the education system is built to create more bricks in the wall (as the famous Pink Floyd song goes) and therefore encourages mediocrity. I am not interested in mediocrity. I want people to be their best and to keep improving what their best is!

I know lots of people with limited formal education who have been extremely successful in business and in what they do. I believe it is important that people constantly build their skills and that they are taught how to manage their 'business'. As I said earlier, when I say 'business' in this sense I mean everything about their lives – and one of the most important things in our lives is managing money. Our current education system does a terrible job of teaching our kids money management. It's little wonder we are all in credit card debt and give in to our impulses when we go shopping.

If you do not have a formal education past high school you might actually be at an advantage to some others who have higher education. Those who have higher education usually accumulate significant debts to achieve that education, and it is likely the amount you need to build to replace your income might be significantly less!

You need to save for what you want

People will often say that you need to save to get what you want. I believe that mindset is extremely limiting, as it encourages you to save money and then spend what you have saved. A better way of thinking about it is to *invest* to get what you want. Hang on, what the hell does that mean?

Say you want a nice sports car. This sports car will cost you $3,000 a month or $36,000 a year to purchase and run. But there are two ways you can own it sooner, rather than saving for it.

Firstly, you can see if there is a way you can monetise owning the car so that you can derive some income from the car. That might be things like taking prospective clients for a drive or to track days to help you close more business deals. You might work out that the car helps you close enough business to earn another $20,000 a year. Yay! Only $16,000 per annum to go.

Secondly, you can have investments providing you with the cashflow to pay for the car.

Why is this so much better than saving?

By doing it this way you will have the cashflow in perpetuity (forever) to keep funding your nice car. Also, by doing it this way you will more than likely be able to structure the purchase to be more tax effective. ☺

If you had just saved for the car you would have paid for the car and then not had the money for the ongoing costs, or the ability to keep funding it forever.

TALL POPPY SYNDROME AND SELF-SABOTAGE

Let's talk about one of the big causes of self-sabotage I come across all the time in my work.

In Australia, we seem to have an issue with tall poppy syndrome. It comes from our underdog mentality. It means we tend to scoff at people who have 'made it' and think that anyone who is doing well for themselves is screwing everyone else. That is total bullshit. If you have this mentality I can guarantee that you are self-sabotaging your own success.

Self-sabotaging your own success means that you are subconsciously limiting yourself because of your ingrained beliefs. You will be doing things based on what you believe that are not helping you towards your financial freedom. If you think wealthy people are crooks you will not let yourself become one because you don't want to be a crook.

Here is my advice: *stop it!*

Part of the tall poppy mentality is believing wealthy people don't pay their 'fair share'. By saying this you are suggesting that being wealthy isn't fair or the right thing to do. If you believe this then you won't allow yourself to become wealthy as it isn't fair or the right thing to do, and because you wouldn't be paying your 'fair share'. This is one of the worst beliefs you can have, as well as being wrong!

Do you know how much tax the wealthy pay? I have some extremely wealthy clients and they pay a lot in tax, even though we help reduce their tax burden substantially. In one year they will pay more than a lot of people pay in their lifetime.

There's a common tongue-in-cheek way in the world of Australian accounting to explain the tax system – in beer.

Imagine if, once a week, 10 football fans who are all members of the same footy club went out for a beer together after the game. The bill for all 10 comes to $100. If they paid their bill the way we pay our taxes, it would go something like this:

- The first four people – the poorest – would pay nothing.
- The fifth would pay $1.
- The sixth would pay $3.
- The seventh would pay $7.

- The eighth would pay $12.
- The ninth would pay $18.
- And the tenth (the richest) would pay $59.

So, that's what they decided to do.

This group of 10 footy fans drank in the bar every week and seemed quite happy with the arrangement until the pub owner caused them a little problem. 'Since you are all such loyal customers, I'm going to reduce the cost of your weekly bill by $20 and your beers will now cost you only $80.'

The group still wanted to pay the bill the way we pay our taxes. So the first four people were unaffected. They would still drink for free, but what about the other six? The paying customers? How could they divide the $20 windfall so that everyone would get their fair share?

They realised that $20 divided by six is $3.33 but if they subtracted that from everybody's share then not only would the first four people still be drinking for free but the fifth and sixth would each end up being paid to drink their beer.

So, the bar owner suggested that it would be fairer to reduce each person's bill by a higher percentage. They decided to follow the principle of the tax system they had been using and proceeded to work out the amounts that each should now pay:

- The fifth person, like the first four, now paid nothing (a 100% saving).
- The sixth now paid $2 instead of $3 (a 33% saving).
- The seventh now paid $5 instead of $7 (a 28% saving).
- The eighth now paid $9 instead of $12 (a 25% saving).

- The ninth now paid $14 instead of $18 (a 22% saving).
- The tenth now paid $50 instead of $59 (a 15% saving).

So, each of the last six was better off than before with the first four continuing to drink for free.

But, once outside the bar, the beer-drinking group began to compare their savings. 'I only got $1 out of the $20 saving!' declared the sixth person, pointing to the tenth person. 'But you got $9!'

'Yes, that's right!' exclaimed the fifth person. 'I only saved $1 too. It's unfair that they got nine times more benefit than me!'

'That's true!' shouted the seventh drinker. 'Why should they get $9 back when I only got $2? The wealthy get all the breaks!'

'Wait a minute!' yelled the first four drinkers in unison. 'We didn't get anything at all. This new tax system exploits the poor!' The nine drinkers then surrounded the tenth and continued to abuse the person further.

The next week the tenth drinker didn't show up for the game or the drinks afterwards, so the nine sat down and had their beers without them. But when it came time to pay the bill, they discovered something important – they didn't have enough money between all of them to pay for even half of the bill.

And that is how our tax system works. The people who already pay the highest taxes will naturally get the most benefit from a tax reduction. Tax them too much and attack them for being wealthy and they might not show up anymore. In fact, they might start drinking overseas, where the atmosphere is somewhat friendlier.

There's good news, though! You can build passive income, and passive income can be invested so that you don't have to pay the highest tax rates but instead pay corporate tax rates or even lower.

BREAKING A NEGATIVE MONEY MINDSET

So, how do we break this negative mindset on money?

It will take work and time if you have these things holding you back.

The first exercise I am going to suggest that you try is to plan out what you would do if you had an unlimited amount of money. I know a lot of you are probably thinking of taking a vacation! If you are thinking like that then I am glad you have this book. I personally wouldn't change much about my life, even if I had unlimited funds; I love what I am doing. My main change would be to get more resources to help spread the work that I do further and help more people.

So, when you are thinking about this, consider the following things. 'What daily tasks would I not do if I could afford not to do them?' Think about the jobs you really don't want to do around the house. I personally haven't mowed for years; I hated mowing so I decided to pay someone to do it. You might not like cleaning, so you would get a house cleaner; you might not like to cook, so you would get an in-house cook. You might not like driving, so you would get a chauffeur (or you could just use Uber, depending on where you live). So, after you have thought about that, think about what you would do with that free time that you have just gained for yourself. Who are you going to help? What are you going to do? Who are you going to give money to? What causes are you going to support? All of a sudden money isn't evil, is it?

If you practise this and remind yourself everyday what you want from that day and what you want to do with your money, you will let money empower you to do the things that help you and those around you. Part of letting money empower you is to speak openly about it with your family. If you want their assistance and want them to join you on this journey it is important that they start to prescribe to similar principles around money as you do.

Something to remember about your money is that it is yours, but everyone is attempting to take their piece of it. All of those ads you see, all of that marketing, all of those things you are being offered are attempting to take a share of your money, so you need to be focused on what you actually want.

If you are reading this book, I doubt you are the kind of person who would sit around and do nothing, even if you had unlimited money. If that is you, maybe this book isn't for you. If you suddenly had unlimited money and you were helping people on a massively bigger scale, giving your time and resources to causes you wanted to and, more importantly, doing the things that you want to do – that is the power of money! It isn't evil; it just is. You determine what you do with it. If you are like most people, you want to help other people – because that is the most fulfilling thing that a human can do.

ACTION POINTS

- Think about what you would do with unlimited money.
- Consider the tasks you would you pay somone else to do.
- List some causes that you would support.
- Stop self-sabotaging. Just stop it! Money isn't evil.

CHAPTER 2

THE ART OF GOAL SETTING

Goal setting is so important that I am dedicating an entire chapter to it. Without goals you have no destination to reach so it is hard to even get started.

Without goals, you have no compass. With no compass, there is no destination. Without a destination, you are just going blindly forward. You don't go somewhere in your car without knowing where you are going, do you? No.

However, it is not enough simply to have goals. There are many things you need to do to increase the probability that you will actually achieve your goals. The problem with just having a goal is it is only the destination. That in itself does not give you a map of how to get there.

I will start by looking at the internal factors that might be holding you back from achieving what you want. I will then explain the external factors that can have an impact on your goals. I'll suggest exercises that can help you get past some of the barriers preventing you from achieving ultimate success. I will then go through some of the best ways to set out your goals so you can achieve that success.

This book is not *only* about goal setting, so I am giving you a summarised version of some great lessons that I have learned along the way.

INTERNAL FACTORS

As we learned in chapter 1, there are things you might be telling yourself that are preventing you from achieving the goals that you want. Let's revisit beliefs. You will never get past the beliefs that you currently have. What I mean by this is that if you think that you are only worth $100,000 per annum, that is all you will ever earn. You have to believe that you are worth $1 million per annum to earn that amount. You need to believe it before you can earn it. Without the belief, you will sabotage yourself as you won't think you are worth it.

It's worth examining your beliefs more closely and identifying whether they are empowering or disempowering beliefs. An empowering belief inspires you to go forward while a disempowering belief holds you back. I hold the belief that if you want something, you can find someone with the resources available to help you get it. It is just a matter of what it will cost you and what you need to give up. I believe that you can have anything you want; the question is whether you are creative enough to find a solution to get it. That is an empowering belief. A disempowering belief is that you don't have the resources to get what you want and you don't think there is any other way of making it happen.

So, what do you do if you have disempowering beliefs that are holding you back? You need to remove them. Unfortunately, beliefs are heavily ingrained in who we are, so it won't happen overnight – but a tactic that can work well is visualisation and verbalisation. Essentially what you want to do is tell yourself a new story. Your beliefs come from the story you tell yourself. So, change the story. Every morning and evening visualise what you want to have and then verbalise your new beliefs. Do this and you will start acting this way as well. It will become your story and your beliefs will have changed.

To help with visualisation some people like to use story boards or keep some of their goals written down in places that they will be able to read/view them regularly. I think that this is a good idea but personally I have found that this can sometimes blend into the background of everything else that you are doing. One of the best things you can do is to try different techniques and figure out what works best for you.

EXTERNAL FACTORS

Now it is time to explore some of the external factors that will help or hinder the achievement of your goals.

Let's start with who you share your goals with. It is important to tell the people who can help you achieve your goals. If a person can't help you with the achievement of your goals then there is no need to tell them about your goals. You need to be careful who you share with as some people will look to bring you down and say that you can't achieve your goals.

The next external factor is the people you are hanging around with. There is a lot of truth in the saying that you are the average of the five people you spend the most time with. If you are hanging around people with negative energy they will infect you with their energy and you will not be able to achieve your goals; but if you hang around people with positive energy, it is simply amazing the things that can be achieved. Positive people just seem to make shit happen.

Finally, one of the most important things you can invest in is having an accountability partner to keep you accountable to your goals (more on this later in the chapter).

HOW TO SET GOALS

The first thing to consider with any goal is that it needs to be a SMART goal. Most people will have heard about SMART goals, but in case you haven't it stands for:

- **S**pecific
- **M**easurable
- **A**chievable
- **R**elevant
- **T**imely/time-bound.

There are a number of variations with very similar meanings, but this is my preference. You need to be able to answer each of these for your goal to have enough meat to it to be able to manage yourself on the way to achieving it.

Here is an example of how it works. Lisa has a goal to pay off her credit card debt of $10,000 over the next 12 months. She is a single person living with flatmates making $100,000 per annum.

- *Is it specific?* Yes, $10,000 debt paid off in 12 months.
- *Is it measurable?* Yes, Lisa can measure how she is paying down that $10,000.
- *Is it achievable?* Yes, I am sure Lisa can find an interest-free balance transfer card and will only have to pay down the principal over the 12 months, rather than any interest. That is only $833.33 per month or $27 a day. It may mean she spends a bit less on beer and wine over the next 12 months but it's definitely achievable.

- *Is it relevant?* Yes, credit card debt is expensive and one of the best things you can do is to pay it off as quickly as possible as a way of achieving financial freedom.
- *Is it time-bound?* Yes, Lisa has 12 months to achieve her goal.

Intangible goals can be turned into SMART goals. Let's say that Luke wants to be a better parent. Saying that he wants to be a better parent is not a SMART goal. However, saying that he will be a better parent by spending at least one hour of quality time per week with each of his children by themselves is a SMART goal.

- *Is it specific?* Yes, one hour per week per child. He could even go one step further with older children and get them to rate him out of 10, and ask them what they would like to do with him for that one hour.
- *Measurable?* Yes, Luke can check if he spent one hour with each child.
- *Achievable?* Yes, Luke could plan to spend less time watching TV allowing him more time for his children.
- *Relevant?* Yes. I think being a better parent should be on all parents' lists of goals. I am not saying that we are all bad parents, just that we should all be striving to improve.
- *Timely?* Yes, Luke can start now and build it into a habit.

Okay, now you have your SMART goal. You have your destination! YAY! Go you. You have completed the first step in achieving your goals. That is the easy part! Now it is time to build your map to achieving your goals.

CREATING YOUR GOAL ROADMAP

So how do you create the roadmap to reaching your goal?

I personally find that the easiest way is to back into your goal. By that I mean you work backwards to figure out what you need to do to get to your goal. In the example earlier, Lisa worked out that she needed to pay just over $27 per day to reach her goal. That is working backwards to the goal. Say it is something more complex. You might want to go into business for yourself. The best thing to do is work out mini goals, which are essentially things that need to be done before you start. For example you might say that you need to have a company setup with a name, and that you want six months' cashflow saved up. Each of these things gives you a mini goal to work towards.

The map doesn't need to be complex; often, the simpler it is the better, and the easier it is to understand. It is important that the mini goals that you create are simple and easy to measure.

Doing this for financial freedom is also easy. You work out what income you want to have without working. You then need to work out how much money you need to have for that to cover the rest of your life. Once you have done this you can then work out how much you need to be saving and investing to achieve this in the shortest time possible.

ACCOUNTABILITY

Now it is time to discuss one of the most important parts of successful goal setting: accountability. Accountability can make or break your chances of achieving your goal.

The Association for Financial Counseling & Planning Education lists the following probabilities of completing a goal:

- You have an idea or goal: 10%
- You consciously decide you will do it: 25%
- You decide when you will do it: 40%
- You plan how you will do it: 50%
- You commit to someone that you will do it: 65%
- You have a specific accountability appointment with a person you've committed to: 95%.

A you can see, even if you have created a roadmap for your goal you are still only at a probability of 50%. That's a one in two chance of failing – pretty bad when you think about it. However, if you have a specific accountability appointment with someone you have committed to your chances of success increase to 95%. Now that is huge. Absolutely *massive*! When I came across this I knew there was only one way to achieve goals and that is by having an *accountability partner*.

What does a good accountability partner actually do for you?

A good accountability partner is there to keep you accountable to what you commit to doing. They are not there to be your friend and are not there to be a shoulder to cry on. A good accountability partner will not give you lovey-dovey crap – they will give you the truth. Whether you like it or not they need to be honest and sometimes brutal in helping you achieve your goals.

A true accountability partner will not allow your excuses to take priority; it is either you did what you said you would, or you didn't. There is no middle ground.

It is important though that your accountability partner has the ability to actually help you achieve your goals. Their main aim should be to help keep you accountable and help you push through your obstacles as they arise.

A good accountability partner should be a sounding block when you come across obstacles, listening to you and providing a different perspective on how to approach your problems to ensure that you get through them successfully.

So, while an accountability partner needs to be honest about your performance they should also be able to provide guidance and assistance to move through obstacles as they come across your path to success. Remember, an accountability partner improves your chances of success exponentially. From one in two to 19 in 20! So, make sure you invest in the right person to help you.

ACTION POINTS

- What are your disempowering beliefs? Write them down and tear them up.

- What are the opposites to those disempowering beliefs? Write them down and start to change your story.

- Develop your SMART goals.

- Work out your roadmap to reach your goals with mini goals.

- Find your accountability partner.

CHAPTER 3

THE BASICS

In this chapter, I am going to redefine assets and liabilities and examine what you need to take control of, and where you should get professional help. I will also describe some basics on accounting so that you can start to own your 'business' – that is, start to be accountable for your own money state. I will be binning the bullshit accounting terms that financial professionals like to use, instead explaining everything in terms that a 10-year-old could understand. (I know because I checked that my actual 10-year-old could understand them.)

So, let's start at the start!

REDEFINING ASSETS AND LIABILITIES

What is an asset? The accounting definition is:

> Things that are resources owned by a person and/or company and which have future economic value that can be measured and can be expressed in dollars. An asset is a resource controlled by the entity as a result of past events and from which future economic benefits are expected to flow to the entity.

Traditionally, things that are considered assets include:

- Car
- House (that you live in)
- Personal contents
- Investments
- Cash
- Superannuation (US readers: 401K or pension funds)
- High-value items such as jewellery, musical instruments and so on.

What is a liability? In accounting:

> Liabilities are the future sacrifices of economic benefits that the entity (person and/or company) is presently obliged to make to other entities as a result of past transactions or other past events.

Traditionally, things that are considered liabilities include:

· Car loan
· House loan
· Credit cards/store cards
· Investment loans
· Money you owe to bill providers
· Other unmet commitments (leases and so on).

I view assets and liabilities a bit differently to the traditional view. I define an asset as an item that provides ongoing cashflow to the owner. A liability is an item that provides negative cashflow to the owner.

Under these definitions, what most people in Australia consider their biggest asset – the house that they live in – is actually a liability. Does it provide you with cashflow? No. Does it cost you money to own? Yes!

What about your car and personal contents? A car is a liability as it takes cash to run and maintain, and most cars depreciate in value. Personal contents is just stuff. We all know it isn't worth what it is insured for because no one values your stuff except you.

I learned about this alternative view of assets and liabilities from businessman and author Robert Kiyosaki.

In summary, assets bring in cash and liabilities take cash. Make sense? If not, read through the start of this chapter again.

This book that you are reading is one of my assets. I wrote it and it generates ongoing cashflow for me. Therefore, it is an asset. Most people wouldn't consider putting a book on their balance sheet but if it is generating cashflow for you then there is no other way of describing it.

Why am I emphasising and using cashflow as my determining factor for defining assets and liabilities?

Simple: cashflow is king! No, that's not a mistake – I didn't say cash is king, I said *cashflow* is king!

WHY IS CASHFLOW KING OVER CASH?

Once you spend cash it is gone. If you have cashflow, though, it just keeps coming! Great cashflow will take care of any poor cash position and at the end of the day that is everything. We all need to live and pay for things and the best way to ensure we can keep doing that is awesome cashflow. Think about the amount of cash you would need to have to pay for your bills for the rest of your life. It earns nothing in the bank and burns a giant hole in your pocket when you have it. (Yes, I am insinuating that we would all love to spend the cash we have.)

Cashflow, though, will give you what you need consistently and if you build it right it can continue to grow. How awesome is that?

So where does cashflow come from? Cash follows assets. In other words, to build cashflow you need to have assets. Unless you are fortunate enough to have parents provide you with wealth you're probably starting with nothing – or even worse than nothing: a lot of us start working with large debts that we owe for getting our higher education. Great system they have working for us, right?! Anyway, it is essential that you start putting away some of your income that you earn from working in a job or from business. This will allow you to build and buy assets that generate cashflow. The more that you can do that, the more you be able to build up your asset base. The faster you build up your asset base, the faster you can build your cashflow. The faster you build your cashflow, the faster you are able to achieve financial freedom by having more cashflow than you need to live your life in the manner you want with the people you want.

This is where it is important to remember a couple of things. Firstly, everyone is after your money – as a result you need to be conscious of how you spend it. Secondly, to ensure you don't buy the stuff that you don't need the best thing that you should do is to pay yourself first. What does that mean?

That means when you get that paycheque (or however you get your money) the first thing you do is put some of that money towards your asset column. Treat it as an expense and put it into that column so that you are able to build those assets and start generating that cashflow. Do that first and you will learn to live within what you leave yourself with. Simple as that.

EXAMPLES OF ASSETS

Let's take a look at some examples of assets. We'll start with some of the more traditional assets.

Real estate

This is a favoured category by many, but not particularly by me. I think this asset class can be done well but most people do not do it well. What do I mean by that? Remember that I see an asset as something that provides cashflow and doesn't take from cashflow. In Australia real estate brings with it a few things that really detract from its attractiveness as a cashflow investment. Those are primarily taxes. While we get some tax benefits from property we are also blessed with having to pay expensive stamp duty on the purchase of the property; and when we own the property we have ongoing costs of rates, insurance, repairs and land tax. Let's also not get started on residential tenants' rights. Land tax in itself can take all of your cash return if you are not careful.

A client of mine had taken care of his finances for his entire life. He was turning 60 the year I was writing this book. He had $7 million worth of real estate with a cashflow from this 'asset' of negative $30,000 per annum. I am not kidding you – it was costing him to have this real estate. Instead of providing him cashflow it was taking cash away! As a result he is now having to liquidate some of the real estate so that he can invest in a cashflow-positive manner.

Real estate can provide exceedingly strong cashflow returns. I have three examples from my own investing to take you through, demonstrating how to generate really good cashflow from real estate. The first example is a commercial building that I purchased with some other people I knew. We fitted it out and leased it out. Our first-year cashflow was 9.8%. We held it for three years and in the last year we were receiving a tax effective 11.2% cashflow and also received a 10% capital gain. (I will explain about adding value later in the book.)

My second example is a commercial property investment that is only made available to sophisticated investors (you'll find out more about becoming a sophisticated investor in chapter 8). In the first year it achieved cashflow returns of 9.4% with only half of that income even being taxable! Not only that, the property improved in value by 10% in the first 12 months.

My last example will give you a final way to think about property. Currently there are regions where you can buy homes that have tenants in them that are paying more in rent than it would cost for them to buy the same home. That's right: rent is more expensive then actually owning the house! These properties are great examples of how you can increase your cashflow.

Shares and listed investments

First let's define what shares and listed investments are. By listed investments I mean any investment that is listed on a stock exchange (for example, the Australian Securities Exchange or the New York Stock Exchange) and is easily traded on these exchanges. Shares are a share in a company. If you have shares in the Commonwealth Bank of Australia you technically own a small part of that business.

I personally prefer liquid investments over illiquid assets such as real estate. A liquid investment is any investment that can easily and quickly be turned into cash. I typically prefer to invest in shares and other listed assets as these are liquid. If you need to liquidate an asset relatively quickly or need to start drawing down on it it's easy to do so if it's liquid (you can't sell 1% of a property).

In Australia the buying and selling costs are also a lot less for liquid investments, and they don't have the same holding costs as other illiquid assets.

In Australia, the companies listed on our stock exchange provide and pay substantial amounts of their profit to shareholders. A big positive when it comes to shares is their tax effectiveness in Australia. Australian shareholders usually get a tax credit with the income that is received. This means that for some taxpayers it actually boosts their income, and for all taxpayers it is a very tax-effective way of getting income.

Globally though shares pay less in income than some other investments so it is important to understand some of the ways to get income from investing in shares – as some of the financial engineers out there (me included) have devised ways of doing this.

There are now different listed investments that concentrate on producing income (some paying 10% per annum). There are also products out there that are attempting to provide substantial returns (up to 20% per annum) while providing some protection to the capital value of your funds. Generally speaking in Australia you have shares paying out 4 to 6% gross income per annum which, at the time of writing, is four to six times what you can get for term deposits in the bank. However, even though dividends are higher than term deposits, over time dividends grow while income from term deposits will not grow – it will change only with interest rates.

Bonds, fixed interest securities and mortgages

First let me explain what bonds and fixed interest securities are – as these assets are often misunderstood in the Australian market.

A bond is a debt issued by a company or government. As an example, you give the government $80 today and in 10 years' time they will give you back $100. This is a fixed interest bond. While this bond is issued at $80, the value of the bond will change if interest rates change. Fixed interest securities can include bonds but also include other similar investments that are usually a loan to a company or institution. Bonds and other investments that are loans to a company or institution can also have a variable interest rate; these are typically more capital stable (they don't move in value) due to the fact that the return changes with changes to interest rates.

There is more than one type of bonds and fixed interest securities, and just because they are bonds and/or fixed interest does not mean that they maintain the same capital value. The majority of bonds and fixed interest securities will change in value during the time that they are held due to the fact that interest rates are changing. If you hold a bond or fixed interest security from the beginning until maturity this doesn't matter, as you will receive the funds you invested back (provided the issuer doesn't go into liquidation/bankruptcy) – but you will see a change in the value.

In Australia we have a range of options to help fit this part of a portfolio. At the time of writing a lot of our banks and insurers have issued hybrid securities that are more like variable interest securities that provide some of the tax benefits of share ownership and can pay gross interest rates of almost 3 to 5% per annum. While there are mortgage products that can provide 4 to 7% per annum in the current market, term deposits are paying less then 1.5% per annum. This is an important part of any investment strategy, as the key is to help leverage some of the income.

Now let's explore some non-traditional assets that you can consider.

Intellectual property

In this new, exciting world we cannot ignore the fact that you can build your own assets with little to no money and can get them to start working for you. Some of the things that you can build are online courses, books, podcasts and even YouTube channels. All of these can provide an income and are in a sense a type of business.

Some of these options might not bring in large amounts of income, but some people have built careers out of them and they can be designed to provide income in perpetuity. These are a different style of asset from what you might normally consider, but it is important to understand that if you decide to make/build any of these things they are an asset for you.

Business ownership

If you decide to buy or start a business it is important to understand that you have just bought an asset, or you are trying to build one. A great business is a business that will operate without you and provide an ongoing source of income. Unfortunately, a poor business can become more of a liability then an asset. Small to medium businesses can provide the greatest return on your funds invested. They carry a risk that if managed will make sure you get great ongoing returns as the business thrives.

A great business operation will provide substantial returns far superior to other types of investments, but they do have a different profile. You will require professional advice if you are looking at starting or investing in a business.

HOW TO KNOW IF YOU ARE MAKING MONEY

If you have made it this far into the book, you know that I believe you need to take care of your own 'business'. What I mean by this is that you take care of your own personal and family finances and that you learn the basics of what you are working through and on. Part of this means learning and understanding some basics of accounting.

At the start of this chapter I spoke about the definitions of assets and liabilities. Unfortunately due to the restrictions placed on accountants they aren't going to change the way they define assets and liabilities for you (I should know – I am one). So how do you figure out what is happening with your money, and whether you are actually making money?

As you are primarily concerned with cashflow you need to start with a cashflow statement. The best thing about a cashflow statement is that it only shows you cash in and out so you know what your cash position is like month in, month out.

Opposite is an example monthly cashflow statement so you can see how to put one together.

Taxes paid is kept separate in this example as the tax is paid before the wages and investment income are received.

This cashflow statement isn't something your accountant or financial planner is likely to prepare for you. You need to take care of your 'business' and start doing this for yourself, or find a professional who can help in a similar way.

Monthly cashflow statement for Jim and Jane

Incoming cash – from work	
Wages 1	$5,114
Wages 2	$5,114
	$10,228
Incoming cash – from assets	
Investment portfolio	$300
Net rental income	$800
	$1,100
Total income	**$11,328**

Expenditure – for personal living	
Basic living expenses	$3,300
Discretionary expenses	$2,000
Mortgage	$3,300
	$8,600
Expenditure – investments	
Investment portfolio – margin loan	$100
Rental mortgage	$2,000
	$2,100
Total expenses	**$10,700**

Savings/(deficit)	$628
Taxes paid	$2,972

The cashflow statement is the starting point because without positive cashflow you are done. You cannot sustain negative cashflow indefinitely.

But does having positive cashflow mean you are making money?

No, not necessarily – which is why you also need to have a profit and loss statement. Unfortunately, a traditional profit and loss doesn't correlate very well with cashflow. Profit does not equal cash. I can tell you right now I have seen more than one business go under even though they were very profitable. Being profitable doesn't pay the bills, cashflow does. Ideally, profit should lead to more cash. Where people come unstuck is where they are worrying about the value of what they are creating without thinking about the cashflow they currently have. This can sometimes result in people getting stuck in a situation where they have the opposite of what they wanted.

Let's look at an example of what I am talking about.

We'll begin with negatively geared property in Australia. Negatively geared property is property that is losing money every year – from a tax perspective, at least. A property in Australia could be negatively geared due to a couple of reasons. Firstly, it is most likely losing money. The other reason is due to the depreciation claims that are allowed in Australia. When you are looking at property as an investment in Australia you are allowed to claim the majority of the costs of the property including interest on borrowings and depreciation on improvements and the building. Now, if you have an investment property that is negatively geared because of the claim on the building and improvements, this could assist you in creating a cashflow-positive asset – as the property is making money, but losing money for tax purposes, providing you further cashflow from tax rebates.

Let's look at an example to illustrate this. Say you are buying a $1.6 million house. You spend $320,000 on the deposit plus another $100,000 in stamp duty and other costs. Mortgage repayments are $5,390 per month with ongoing costs of about $100 per week. That is $1,244 per week in mortgage repayments plus other ongoing costs. Compare that to renting the same property for $890 per week and that is 354 extra in cash outflow if you are renting rather than owning. Now, if you own this property as an investment you have to be able to fund this cashflow on your investment. You might be able to receive a tax deduction on this amount but you are still a long way from being cashflow positive on the property. If you do this on 10 properties then you end up with a lot of investments that are just costing you cash.

Investing like this can make your assets look great but that is no good if your cashflow is stuffed.

Compare this to a diversified growth portfolio (a portfolio of diverse liquid investments built for long-term growth) of $1 million. I am using $1 million in this example as you are able to get some leverage on this size of portfolio and use the rest as a deposit. The interest rate will be higher, but in terms of cashflow this investment will give you equity of $420,000 (no stamp duty or start-up costs) and after that you can expect to get a cash return of $25,243, and you can also expect a tax return even if you're at the highest marginal tax rate.

If you had just invested the $420,000 you would be able to get $24,000 in cashflow.

Here is an example of an investment profit and loss statement.

Investment profit and loss for Jim and Jane

Income	
Investment portfolio – cash	$300
Net rental income	$800
	$1,100

Expenses	
Interest – investment portfolio	$100
Interest – rental property	$1,600
	$1,700

Net income before taxes	**-$600**
Investment portfolio – tax paid credits	$60
Investment property – tax benefit on non-cash item	$143.75
Net income after taxes	**-$396.25**

In summary, it is important to take stock and work out what assets and liabilities you really have. Do you even have any assets that are working for you? Do you have any investments that are costing you (or your cashflow), or are they generating cashflow for you?

Understand the different assets that you can own and find what works for you. The goal is to build your cashflow. There is no wrong way to do this, but the key thing is to understand the cashflow that different assets will generate.

Make sure that you build and understand your profit and loss. Be a boss and take control. Start measuring your cashflow today and start managing it to improve it.

ACTION POINTS

- Take stock. What assets and liabilities do you really have?

- Consider which asset class you like best, and why. Do some research on the asset classes you currently invest in and those you might consider.

- Build your cashflow. Do you have any positive cashflow apart from income earned through work?

- Build your profit and loss. Do you have any investments?

- Start investing today!

CHAPTER 4

MONEY ALLIES: DEBT AND PROFESSIONAL HELP

There are plenty of allies you can make use of as you start to take control of your money. This chapter focuses on two of them: debt (used wisely), and professional help.

Let's start by exploring how to make debt your ally. You have to be careful with debt, as it can help or hinder you.

Most people will use debt in their lifetime – whether it's to buy a house or a car, or even just the very cheap government-funded student loans we get in Australia. Let me start by stating that there is nothing wrong with using debt as long as it is used for the right purposes.

Let's take a look at some of the different types of debt.

PERSONAL DEBT

Personal debt includes things like credit cards, personal loans and car loans. This is the bad stuff. It is the devil that you should never keep. I am all for using a credit card to get those rewards points but you better make sure that you pay it off every month. If you don't have the discpline to do that then credit cards aren't worth it.

Personal loans are the worst. If you have these the best thing you can do is pay them off as quickly as possible. Compound interest works both ways and in personal loans it works terribly against you.

HOME DEBT

This is debt incurred for the purchase of your home. As long as it makes sense there isn't anything particuaraly wrong with this type of debt. The problem I see too often with this type of debt is that people redraw against it for the wrong reasons – for that new boat or new car – instead of it being used as a source of cashflow to build investment nest eggs. Be careful with this type of debt; the banks are happy to keep lending to you forever on this type of asset. Also, since the debt is for your personal home it isn't likely to be tax deductible, so you will want to pay the debt down as quickly as possible.

SECURED DEBT

Secured debt is incurred for purchase of cars, equipment and other items. The purpose of the item and how it is purchased determines whether it is good debt or bad debt. If you're running a business that needs equipment, the debt makes sense as it will provide lower interest rates than unsecured debt. If you use secured debt to buy a personal car (not via tax effective means) this is not the best use of debt, and on top of that you are most likely paying higher rates of non-deductible interest (as per personal debt).

BUSINESS DEBT

It doesn't matter what you do in business – debt for business is a guarantee. As soon as you start collecting money you start owing money to someone. There is nothing wrong with business debt as long as it is used for its purpose. An overdraft should only be used to deal with cashflow timing issues and gaps between when you have to make payments and when you receive payments. Equipment finance should be used to purchase equipment that is actually needed for the business. There are two debts that you don't want to accrue when you are in business: superannuation debt for employees, and debt owing to the tax office. As soon as you start accruing those it becomes very difficult to borrow money.

INVESTMENT DEBT

This is the best type of debt you can have, as it helps you purchase investments to generate wealth and cashflow for you. Using this debt in the right way will give you enhanced returns over the long term and help increase your cashflow.

It is important, though, to understand the difference between a debt repayment and an interest repayment. Too often people come to me and think they can claim their full loan repayment on an investment property as a tax deduction, when they can only claim the interest component.

MAKING DEBT WORK FOR YOU

So how do you get the most out of debt to help with your cashflow? First let's explore the different types of payment options you can have, and how they might work for you.

Interest only

This is a loan where you pay off the interest incurred on the debt, rather than making any headway towards paying off the debt balance. The trap with interest only is that you will not actually ever pay down the debt. This is a real problem if you have high leverage (that is, if the debt on your investments is greater than 50%).

The issue can be that you will never have much equity to ensure that the cashflow from your investment is significant. Interest only can work well with instalment/savings plans. This is when you are consistently borrowing while also providing equity to an investment. You might contribute $1,000 of your own funds and borrow $500 a month. When doing this it can make sense to pay interest only, while your debt continues to grow.

Principal and interest

This is the ideal way to pay down debt as the debt balance will reduce over time. This gives you greater equity over time and ensures that your investments will provide greater free cashflow over the long term. The issue with principal and interest is that it will take some of your cashflow to pay down your debt which you could use to invest in other ways.

*

As you can see there is no right or wrong answer on how you actually address your debt, and this is why it is important to consider how you are investing to choose the right debt.

Let's take a look at some examples of using investment debt in the right way.

Jack buys a commercial property for $500,000 with 70% leverage – that is, the bank is providing $350,000 towards the purchase price. The property pays cashflow (yield) of 7.8% ($39,000) per annum. The interest rate on the debt is 5.5%. Jack paid a deposit of $150,000 plus other costs of $30,000. The cashflow on an interest-only loan for this property would provide Jack with $19,750 per annum – more than 10% of the money Jack invested. The cashflow for a principal and interest loan over 15 years for this property provides $4,680 before tax (Jack even gets a refund due to depreciation claims). The interest provides a tax break on the investment, and taking on the debt allows Jack to access a better investment that he may not have been able to access otherwise, giving him a better return.

Jill decides on an instalment gearing/savings plan – 50% (that is, borrowing 50% of the investment amount) using a diversified growth portfolio paying 6% gross income (including tax credits). Investing the amount of $20,000 per annum of her own money and $20,000 per annum of borrowed funds over a 20-year period, Jill has an investment of $1 million. She receives cashflow in the first year of $2,353.75 which she can choose to reinvest. Furthermore, the tax rules on this type of investment mean that Jill pays minimal to no tax over the investment period.

GETTING THE MOST OUT OF PROFESSIONAL HELP

When you're looking at any long-term investment strategy it is important to get professional help to get the most out of your funds.

Let's take a look at the types of professional help available and what to look for.

Accountant

You will need an accountant at a minimum to help you manage your taxes. They will be also able to explain and provide recommendations on how to minimise your taxes and help with the structuring of your affairs to achieve the best outcome from a tax perspective.

Financial adviser or coach

I prefer the term 'financial coach' to 'adviser', as a coach will help you build a plan, execute that plan and hold you accountable to that plan. That is what a great financial adviser will do for you. They will help coach you through your investment journey including helping you manage your cashflow and referring you to the other appropriate professionals when needed. Great financial coaches also come up with more unique investment opportunities that may not be available on the retail market without the help of a professional.

What I would look for in a financial adviser or coach is someone who will take advantage of everything available to work the system for you, rather then you working for the system. More than that they will be able to provide ongoing support ensuring that you stay on track. They should begin by looking at what you want and then see where you are heading and give you a brief as to how to bridge the gap between the two.

They should be able to work with your accountant from the beginning to ensure that you end up with the best setup, and to show you your cashflow and profit and loss regularly.

Lawyer

Blood-sucking lawyers (sorry to all those lawyers) are vitally important and the more wealth you accumulate the more you will need them. If you decide real estate investing is the way to go you will need someone to help with the acquisition, and someone to help with any leases on commercial properties. As your wealth continues to build you will need to use your lawyer to ensure assets are passed effectively to the next generation.

*

Using these professionals in tandem with each other will help ensure you get the most out of what you have and you are able to protect what you build and get the most out of it.

ACTION POINTS

- Learn about the different types of debt so you understand them.

- Take stock. What type of debt do you have? Do you need to remove any debt?

- Work out what type of debt you can use to help you.

- Consider the advisers you currently work with. Do you need to change any of them? Are there other professionals you need to add to your team of allies?

CHAPTER 5

INTRODUCING THE MONEY BUCKETS

The concept of money buckets is where budgeting begins. Money buckets are a simplified way of looking at your money, and will help you hold onto more of it.

I like to have three separate money buckets into which I allocate certain funds:

· Living
· Fun (discretionary)
· Wealth.

In this chapter I'll define by what I mean by each of these buckets and how I recommend classifying different items in each category.

LIVING

What gets classified as a living expense? Living expenses are what I consider your non-negotiables. It is things such as your groceries, basic utilities, basic mobile phone and internet and can include running costs of cars. Sometimes it's easier to define living expenses by thinking about what *doesn't* go into living bucket. There are a number of things that I believe belong in the fun (discretionary) bucket, and not in the living bucket. Think of the living bucket as containing the things you need for the minimum level of living required.

FUN (DISCRETIONARY)

So, what belongs in the fun bucket? Everything that you don't really need to buy, but you do. That lunch date that you have with your friend every week should go in this bucket. So should going on a holiday; paying for the hobbies you enjoy; taking the kids to one of those play centres; buying that latest phone or car; and going to see the latest *Star Wars* movie. These all fall under the fun category of spending.

Now, it is important for me to remind you that it is important to have fun. One of the goals of this book is to help you create better balance so you can have a great lifestyle and continue it years into the future. So don't think the fun bucket is off limits!

WEALTH

Your wealth bucket is anything that is going to help improve your cashflow now or in the future. Things that can be considered as contributions to your wealth bucket include your mortgage payments (in excess of rent for a similar property), and any contributions to your superannuation or other investments that help build your wealth. In Australia we have the advantage that our employers are mandated to contribute 10% per annum to superannuation for us. That makes a huge difference to what we will have when we are able to access it (at age 60 for most readers of this book); but this book is about how to build investments and wealth separate to that so you can start reaping the benefits a lot sooner than 60.

ALLOCATING FUNDS TO YOUR BUCKETS

Now let's talk about the allocations to these buckets. Ideally you should allocate a third of your income to each of these buckets. That is, if you have $10,000 per month you would put $3,333.33 into each of these buckets. That said, there is a little wiggle room – the truth is that you are probably never going to be able to divide your money by exactly one third into each bucket. My family uses this method to help allocate and track expenditure, and we have 36% of our income going towards wealth, 31% towards discretionary spending and 33% towards living. So, as you can see, it isn't an exact science – but one third is intended to be a good guideline on what to do.

The first thing that you need to do is to work out what your money buckets actually look like. Where is your money going and how are you using it? Doing this gives you the baseline on where you are starting from. You might find that your entire wealth portion is going towards your mortgage and you aren't allowing anything for other wealth-building items. You might find that you are spending a lot on discretionary items including eating out. A 2017 ABS study found that the average Australian household is spending $80 a week eating out. Younger people (which includes me) are spending a $100 a week! While this study is a few years old, I doubt that this has fallen, with the growth of Uber Eats, Deliveroo, Menulog and other delivery apps. That is a fair chunk of change over a year. I think us millennials might have to slow down on the café avocado toast! 😊 Some of things that I have done are, instead of taking the kids to the play centre, I take them to the park; when I catch up with friends we may make our own food. There are plenty of community barbeques you can use.

Remember, you want to get out of the rat race and get onto the fast track, so don't get struck with middle-class fever. Middle-class fever means 'keeping up with the Joneses' – buying that boat, that fast car, those toys and all that other useless shit that I am sure you don't use but thought was a good idea at the time. It is when you buy things and call them assets even though you know (since reading chapter 3) that they are liabilities. These types of purchases take up space. You have to maintain them, you trip over them, you have to pick them up, you have to tidy them up and they just get in the way. I think a great one is kids' toys. Most of them are a waste of money – have you seen how much fun kids can have with recyclables, and what they can make? It is simply amazing. Also, kids don't remember stuff – they remember experiences. The same goes for adults you might buy gifts for: people remember how they feel, not so much what you buy for them, because there is always more shit you can buy.

I am not saying that you can't go and buy stuff you want. But instead of going out and buying it without thought, start considering it differently. If you want a boat, think 'How can I get wealth to pay for my boat?' If you want an $80,000 boat, you might find that it will cost $10,000 per annum with regular updates. So, what you do is you build an investment that pays for that $10,000. Now, that investment might take a few years to grow but once you have built it you won't ever be paying for your boat – your wealth will be. Depending on how you built that wealth you might also have spent a lot less then $80,000 to get it! By using this method there might be some initial sacrifice but there'll be a serious amount of abundance later, as you will be able to upgrade regularly to the latest boat. The biggest thing with this is to stop worrying about what others have. There is only one person you should be comparing yourself to: that person is who you were yesterday. You should always be trying to be a better version of yourself!

Now, if your buckets currently look nothing like the one third division I expect you are wondering how the hell you will get them in balance. The place to start is to look at where you spend your money and the little things you are doing that you might change. When you start making small changes you might find that you free up a bit of the money you had otherwise been mindlessly spending. If you find that after a couple of months you haven't changed at all I highly suggest getting a professional to help you. As we learned in chapter 4, a great financial coach can keep you super accountable and result in much greater success in terms of what you are wanting to achieve.

Look at your situation right now and figure out what and where you can change and start making it happen. It is within your power. Stop making excuses and get to work!

ACTION POINTS

- Categorise your expenditure into buckets.
- Work out how much you are currently spending per bucket.
- Work out some ways to start balancing your buckets.
- Get help if you need it.
- Get to work and start changing your life.

CHAPTER 6

BECOMING A BOSS BUDGETER

In the previous chapter I outlined the way I recommend allocating your funds, which is a part of budgeting. This chapter will delve into the nitty gritty of why budgeting is so important, and give you some methods you can use to get your budget under control. Read this chapter to find out how to become a super boss champion when it comes to budgeting!

The way I think about budgeting is to consider my family as a mini business. Now, if you asked a business owner if they had a budget and they said no, you would think they were crazy! It really isn't any different for your household expenditure. Of course, many people don't have a budget because they don't allocate the time to do it. It is of course a great practice, as doing a budget really is putting your goals down into a written format which increases your chance of success. It also then provides something that you can hold yourself accountable to.

WHY HAVE A BUDGET?

There are three key reasons why you need to have a budget. Let's take a look at them now.

1. Most of your money is already spoken for long before you get it

What you earn has mostly already been promised to someone else to keep the electricity on, make loan repayments and pay for insurance. Budgeting allows you to think about these expenses in advance and make sure you can honour all your commitments.

Now since we are all honest people and plan to pay these bills it is important to know when they are due, so you can plan on how to pay for all of them.

2. Your day-to-day living money is tricky to track

You will keep some cash in your wallet, you might give some cash to your partner, your children might have some money, and everyone pays for items from different places. Ideally if you can pay for things by card that makes it easier to track. The important thing is to not get bogged down in the detail. You need a simple system that allows you to track the bigger categories of your day-to-day expenses such as fuel for your car, shopping and your discretionary spending expenses.

Remember it is important to look at the bigger picture and overall spending. This is why it is better to identify major items first, and then make allowance for smaller items.

Here's the key: you need a system that is so easy to use that you *keep using it.* There are a number of cashflow-management apps and if you get help from a professional they will probably have a preference. Not only that, most of the banks now have basic software that can help with tracking your expenditure in different categories.

3. It's hard to be a boss and live your live without a budget

The biggest reason why a budget is so important is actually the process of doing a budget. Putting together your budget will highlight a number of ways you might not have realised that you spend your money. It might make you realise you have more money than you thought. You can't be a boss without taking control of your financial life. You have to be mindful (and honest) with your situation, which it is hard to do without a budget.

The real magic happens when you review your budget regularly. Don't get frustrated if you are not meeting your budget in the first few months that you are running it. What you need to do is revisit and adjust your budget to suit your needs. This will allow you to improve how you spend your money and give you better discipline with your funds.

This isn't a diet, this is a change in lifestyle. It takes time to ingrain new habits and make the necessary changes to get the success that you want.

AVOID THESE PITFALLS

There are several universal budgeting concepts that every successful budget will be based on, but it is important that the budget you create is simple, effective and easy to manage for you. If you find it hard to keep on track and review the items, get professional help to keep you accountable and help you learn about your spending habits.

Don't try to use a generic, complex, one-size-fits-all budget. A simple approach makes it easier to stay committed and if you start using a professional they will help keep you on track. Similar to when you are getting healthier, you need to stick with realistic changes – do not expect that you will easily make big wholesale changes, such as no more eating out if you are currently eating out five times a week.

While you're going through the process of setting up your budget you might start wondering, why do we like to buy a bunch of shit we don't need? The answer is that buying things can be addictive. Getting deals can feel like a little win. Smart marketers know this, of course, and use it to make us want to buy stuff. Despite this, we hate being sold to, hence we don't like the proverbial dodgy used-car salesman. We want to buy, we like to buy and we want it to feel like it is our idea. This is why discipline in budgeting is so important, as it helps to reduce the amount of shit we don't need making it into our lives.

ZERO-SUM BUDGETING

So now let's get into the nitty gritty of budgeting. Let's look first at zero-sum budgeting, which is a type of budgeting I often recommend. Zero-sum budgeting involves 'spending' every dollar that you make. You are not 'spending' your money in the usual sense, though – you are allocating your entire earnings into appropriate categories. Let's go through the steps you take to run a zero-sum budget.

Step 1: Determine your single or combined total salary

For those who are earning a stable income this is a pretty simple thing to do. You might have to put in a bit more effort if you're not paid a regular amount. If your earnings are irregular, you can attempt to average out a conservative amount that you are paid monthly. Using this method will allow you to start thinking about putting away money so that you have the funds to pay next month's bills with this month's income. By always being 'one month ahead' you will find your budget much easier to plan and keep track of.

Step 2: Itemise your bills

Now that you know the total amount of money coming in, the next step is to work out how much is needed to spend next month on bills, groceries, everyday expenditures and so on. Don't forget your yearly and quarterly expenses. Include everything you can think of as the more accurate it is, the better your budgeting will be. See the list below as an example:

- Mortgage: $1,426
- Fuel/miscellaneous: $200
- Electricity: $200 (estimate)
- Mobile phone: $55
- Gas: $25 (estimate)
- Internet: $35
- Groceries: $500
- Life insurance: $77.31 (paid quarterly)
- Childcare: $500
- Rubbish: $56.25 (paid quarterly)
- Health insurance: $377

  Total: $3,451.56

Step 3: Compare and contrast

Now that you have listed your income and expenses, you will be able to calculate how much is left over. How is this money currently being used? This is where you might realise that you should have more left over then you do, and now you get to work out how you are spending it.

Step 4: Make a choice and stick to it

Once you know how much excess cashflow you have, you can decide what you would like to do with that extra money. You might decide to pay off some debts, save, invest or put it towards a financial goal you have. The only trick is – if you decide to allocate a certain amount of money somewhere, stick to your decision. Put it there straight away and leave it be.

If a couple had a net income of $7,000 for the month, a zero-sum budget may look like this:

- Mortgage: $1,426
- Fuel/miscellaneous: $200
- Electricity: $200 (estimate)
- Mobile phone: $55
- Gas: $25 (estimate)
- Internet: $35
- Groceries: $500
- Life insurance: $77.31 (paid quarterly)
- Childcare: $500
- Rubbish: $56.25 (paid quarterly)
- Health insurance: $377
- Short-term savings: $1,500
- Long-term savings: $1,500
- Holiday fund: $548.44
  Total: $7,000.00

Step 5: Keep on top of your spending

It's important to review your spending month to month and even throughout the month (especially when you are starting out) to make sure you are not spending over your limits. Stick to the motto that 'when it's gone, it's gone'. It may be painful in the first few months, but it can be one of the best ways to create good habits.

Step 6: Make adjustments

It can take a few months before your zero-sum budget is working efficiently. Don't worry about having to make adjustments – it's all part of the budgeting process. As with anything, you will get better at noticing which areas you may need to allocate some more funds to, or where you can easily shave a few dollars off here and there.

OTHER BUDGETING OPTIONS

I am a big fan of zero-sum budgeting – it is a great way for most people to budget – but for those who are a bit more adventurous, I have a few more things to help push you further.

Whichever method you choose, you need to start with what you are paid.

You then work out how much you need to get to your financial goal that you have set. Let's say you have an income of $7,000 per month, similar to the example above, and you work out that you need to spend $4,000 per month to get to your financial goal. Put that $4,000 towards achieving your goal as the first thing you do that month.

Now work out your minimum commitments.

'Hang on!' you might say. 'There isn't enough left to pay my bills or to live!'

You are right! That is the point!

I said this is for those who are more *adventurous*. Let me explain how this can work out.

First of all, you have to have the attitude that once it is gone, it is gone. In the example that we are using you will be short about $500 per month. So, the first thing to do is to look at your spending. What do you have in your life that doesn't improve your life? Whatever you find, remove it immediately. Keep an eye out for things you might be paying for that you aren't using. A good way of getting rid of things you aren't using in this subscription-based world is to change your credit card or debit card and see who starts asking for money. The prompt will get you thinking about the value you get out of these providers that you are paying every month. This is going to be different for everyone as some people will value some things more then others. Personally, I value Spotify highly as I use it a lot – I used it to help write every word in this book. Others however might not value what Spotify does for them and could be fine using the free version.

So what happens if you do that and you still find that you are short? Oh no! (Or is it oh yeah!? ☺)

This is where you really get to work. I personally love doing this as it lines up with something that has been mentioned numerous times within this book which is *to pay yourself first*. Now you have done that you will make sure that you get what you need.

This method will force you into the corner to start getting creative. You will come up with all sorts of ways to make a bit of extra money to cover the hole that you have left to fill. You will force yourself to think outside of the box to find ways to generate the extra income to cover the amount of 'bills' you have and before you know it, you will have done it. You will find a way to cover that shortfall and you will wonder what you were fussing about.

I personally love this method and enjoy being in the situation of trying to make it work out. I love a challenge and have lived with using this method for the majority of my adult life. You can always find a way to make it work and it is great way to push yourself if you are up for the challenge!

Now, this method isn't specifically mine – I first come across it in Robert Kiyosaki's book *Rich Dad Poor Dad*, and have seen different versions of it since. Also, I will say that it isn't for everyone. It is only for the *bold* – those who are willing to work at it hard to make sure that they can still meet their commitments.

Now that I've taken you through the basics of budgeting, let's look at what else you can do with the extra cashflow your budget will create.

ACTION POINTS

- Commit to setting up a budget.

- Work out a system that works for you.

- Compare and review your budget to your actual spending regularly.

- Ask for professional help if needed.

- Pay yourself first.

CHAPTER 7

CASHFLOW DIVERSIFICATION

Cashflow diversification is nothing more then having your wealth spread across multiple avenues for further wealth creation. It's making sure your eggs are not all in one basket.

Let me show you a common example of this. If you have a job and you are earning pay every week, fortnight or month and that is your only income, do you think you have diversification of cashflow? The answer is no, you don't. If you lose that income, all of a sudden you have no income. Don't feel bad if you are in this situation. Even most self-employed people only have one source of income. Most people are like this – they have no diversification of cashflow. This is what I want to inspire people to fix. Diversification of cashflow provides the ultimate security.

There are many ways you can diversify. You can diversify your assets, you can diversify your income streams, you can diversify your friends – diversification applies to literally anything. What I am going to be concentrating on is the diversification of assets (to produce cashflow) and the diversification of income streams (multiple ways you might produce income).

Possibly one of the greatest things about building diversity in your assets and income is that it can help secure your legacy in the future by ensuring that you have income and assets continuing on.

DIVERSIFYING YOUR ASSETS

Let's start with the traditional way to diversify wealth: diversifying your assets.

As an adviser, I split assets into two broad categories: defensive assets and growth assets.

Defensive assets are generally the type of assets that produce some income with little to no growth potential, but they are less volatile in their value and produce lower returns. These are generally things like cash, fixed interest, bonds and so on.

Growth assets are designed to do what they suggest – they grow your wealth. They typically do this with a mixture of income, and growth in the value of the asset (capital growth). They can be volatile in their value day-to-day but have the ability to generate substantially higher returns. They generally include assets such as shares, property, other real estate and other alternative investments. Due to the growth nature of these assets the income they produce along with their value can increase substantially over time.

So, the question to consider is what is going to be the way to go for you? Let me say that you will never be fully invested in only growth assets. It is just impractical. You need to be able to access cashflow day-in day-out. So, you will always have some defensive assets such as cash in a bank account.

I'll now walk through a few examples of how each of these assets performs over time and some of the considerations that you need to make.

First let's start with bonds, which we touched on in chapter 3. The volatility in bond prices depends on the bonds that you have invested in. Bonds move in value as interest rates change in markets. If you hold a bond to maturity you will get your money back – provided the company that issued the bond doesn't default – but it will move in value due to changes in interest rates, unless it is a variable-rate bond. All that means is that the interest rate on the bond changes with the market, so that you will get the market rate plus usually some markup. Other factors can impact the value of a bond too – during times of crisis, safe bonds go up in value while bonds that are perceived as riskier can lose value very quickly. There have been times that people have pushed bonds into accepting negative interest rates.

Another option is to keep money in a bank account or in term deposits. This is probably the safest place you can keep your money for capital preservation. But how safe is it really? I am not talking about losing the money in there – in Australia we have government guarantees, so the chances of losing money are extremely low. I am talking about the low returns applicable, which brings in the issue of inflation risk. That is, over time your money will be worth less than when you initially 'invested' it. If you take any 20-year period you will see that equity returns (and their income returns) have substantially outperformed bonds and cash. The issue with cash as an investment is that the low returns result in its real value declining over time. So how safe is cash as an investment over the long term?

Residential real estate is another option. In Australia at the moment rental yields have become as low as 1% taking costs into account. While looking at Australian equities the yield at the time of writing is 5.2% taking franking credits into account. Franking credits are tax credits that you receive with dividends from Australian companies that have paid tax. They are essentially prepaid tax on the investment that is then treated the same when you complete your tax return. I have no issues with Australian residential property as an investment; my only concern is that due to the investment amount it can be very difficult to build diversity in your cashflow. If you have $2 million in property you might have one to five properties in your portfolio. If something happens to one of those properties it will have a large impact on your income. Property also doesn't provide the liquidity of equity investments and hence is not as volatile.

Okay, so back on point to working out what is right for you. There isn't any one-size-fits-all approach. It really is dependent on what you want to achieve. It is also important to understand that, depending on how aggressive you want to be, you must be willing to lose some money during the process. The purpose of diversification is to help deal with some of the risks that come with investing and being able to weather them due to building in that diversification.

All about risk

Let's look at some of the risks that are involved when you are investing that can have a large impact on your investment.

Inflation risk is particularly important when looking at being defensive with your portfolio. Inflation means that $1 today is not worth $1 tomorrow. Over time the value of money falls and the problem that you can encounter is that inflation (reduction in the value of money) is greater then the returns that you are getting, which results in the real value of your funds decreasing.

Sequencing risk is most important when you are looking at investing a large sum in growth assets in one go. Sequencing risk is the risk that something may happen to cause the value of your investment to fall substantially at the beginning of your investment term.

Drawdown risk is a risk you face when you are at a point in your life where you need to start selling or drawing down on your assets to live. It is the risk of having to draw down on assets when they have fallen in value. It means that you are selling assets when the market is down, which is the worst time to be selling.

Drawdown risk is a particular issue for those who are in unitised superannuation funds. What do I mean by unitised superannuation funds? The cheaper superannuation funds use a unitised model. What that means is that you invest in units to get investments in a variety of different investment classes. This is by itself not necessarily bad. However, when it comes to drawing down for a pension it becomes a real issue. All of the income in these units is reinvested back into the unit itself. This means even if you can separate defensive and growth units the income in the growth units reinvests back into the growth units. This results in only one outcome for people who are drawing down: that is, they have to be drawing down on their growth assets. This is the last thing that you want to be doing when you are at this time in your life, especially if there is a fall in the market. You want your income from your growth assets going to your defensive assets and you want to be drawing down on your defensive assets not your growth assets. The best way to tell if you are in this style of fund is to review your transaction list for your superannuation fund and see if transactions are expressed in both a unit value and cash value. If you still aren't sure I would suggest speaking to an appropriately trained accountant or financial adviser.

Good diversification and good advice can help mitigate these risks. Drawdown risk can be mitigated via appropriate planning and adopting a strategy to ensure income generated goes to the defensive side of your portfolio. Sequencing risk can be mitigated by investing over time and in stages rather then all at once. As I have stated before by paying yourself first on a regular basis you will be investing on a regular basis and will not be as vulnerable to sequencing risk as someone who invests all in one hit.

Rebalancing and reviewing

You may have heard of the concept of rebalancing your portfolio. This is something you can do with your investments provided that they are liquid. The concept is pretty simple. When you started, you would have selected an ideal asset allocation between defensive and growth assets. What rebalancing does is gets you back to that ideal asset allocation. Advisers argue about how often this should be done, but we all agree that it *should* be done. In my opinion you should look at rebalancing your portfolio every 12 months, and no more often than every six months. Sometimes you will find at the 12-month mark your portfolio will still be in balance. The main reason to rebalance is if your growth assets have improved in value or fallen in value. The reason rebalancing works well is that you end up selling growth assets when they are higher in value and buying them when they are low. This means rebalancing is an automatic way of buying low and selling high. Booyah!

It is also important to remember that you need to review your circumstances regularly. If you feel that any adjustments are needed to your portfolio due to changes in your circumstances, you must make them. Remember, you are not necessarily stuck with your investments how they started out – you can build on your portfolio and change how you are investing. It is your money and it is your 'business' so make sure you take ownership and responsibility for what happens with it! Of course, professional advice can help guide you to making the right decisions for yourself, but the buck stops with you.

Ultimately, building diversification into your portfolio to provide the income that you want and having that cashflow coming in is one of the greatest ways to build diversification. Having incoming cashflow and available cash means that you will not need to draw down on growth assets at the wrong time.

DIVERSIFYING YOUR INCOME

In a similar way to building a portfolio of diverse investment assets, you can also build an income stream from multiple sources. In chapter 3 I shared some ideas about how you can build income streams from your intellectual property: you can make money from books, courses and podcasts, and there are many other ways to create passive income sources.

Courses can be a great way to generate income from what you know. People are willing to pay for good content that inspires them to put in the effort to improve themselves. Courses can be a great way to get paid well for what you know when you find your niche.

Podcasts have exploded in popularity and I think this is because of the smartphone and its portability, as well as the fact that people like audio as it allows them to multitask. If you compare audio to video you will find that busy people prefer audio simply because video demands that they sit and watch. Reading a book is similar: you have to block out everything else so you can sit there and read. With audio however you can listen while you are cooking, while you are exercising, while you are driving, while you are doing lots of different things and therefore it is hugely valuable to people. This is why Amazon is dominating with Audible.

If you're creating intellectual property assets you also have to be conscious of what you consider 'success' to be. If you publish a book and it is able to generate $600 a month for you in royalties, is that success or failure? Depending on how much you have decided that you need, that might make a big impact on your finances. Remember, these types of assets will also keep working for you over time.

One of my favourite ways to diversify cashflow is to own multiple businesses. When you buy shares in a company you own part of a business. Owning different businesses is similar but you might own a substantial stake in a smaller business. You can of course start your own businesses and build them from the ground up.

You might be thinking that businesses require effort and they might not work. You are right – they do require effort and they might not work – which is why the rewards can be so much higher then traditional investing.

That said, businesses do have a high failure rate so it's important that you invest in either an established strong small business or you are taking an educated risk with your investment. The advantage of buying into a smaller business is that it will be substantially cheaper than buying into a listed business. Of course, there are many downsides, but the upsides can be substantially greater. If you are considering investing in a smaller business you will be looking to get a return in excess of 30% per annum. For a more established business that might fall to 20%. As you can see there can be great returns for investing in the right business and right people. It takes due diligence and patience but it can be worth it.

I'm often asked, 'What are the best businesses to buy?' There isn't any real benchmark for what the best business is to buy.

My suggestion is to start with a business in an industry that you understand. The next step is to make sure that it is a worthy enough business for your time and money. Every industry has bad, good and great businesses. The key is to stay away from the bad businesses and if you can, invest in the great businesses.

What about starting your own business? This is probably one of the hardest things to do. You will find you will need to learn and grow along the way and that your skills – particularly leadership skills – will be tested to the limit if your goal is to build a sustainable business that can continue to grow without you. However, once you have done it once there is nothing stopping you from starting multiple businesses. Not only that, your role could just be in helping someone else get the money to get started in business, which means you do not necessarily need to be the one doing all the legwork to get the business off the ground.

The beauty of building multiple income streams is that if one of them stops working for you, that is okay – you have other sources of income that you are generating. If you're building a business it is also important to ensure you have multiple sources of income to improve sustainability into the future. There is constant change in business, so it is important that if one well dries up you have others that you can get water from.

*

So, you might now be wondering what the best option is for you when it comes to diversification. My advice is that if you are in the position to diversify both your assets and your income you should do that. If you are in business now you should be working to make sure that business is sustainable without you as quickly as possible. Not only that, you should be looking to grow your wealth independently of the business with different investment assets. If you can, you should also be looking to build intellectual property assets.

If you aren't in business, start investing now. Also, start looking at other ways of bringing in income rather then just your job. See what else you can do with your skills to help build either passive income or a substantial increase in your earned income.

ACTION POINTS

- Consider the diversity you currently have in assets and income, if any.

- List some ways that you can diversify.

- Think about some of the risks that you are or aren't taking. Are you willing to change?

- Plan how you could apply your skills to create intellectual property assets.

- List some other ways you could bring in income.

CHAPTER 8

INCREASING THE MONEY IN YOUR BUCKETS

Let's spend some time looking at how you can increase the money in your money buckets. There are a number of ways to do this outside of just increasing your income. While your income is important, what is more important is how much of that money you get to keep.

One of the most important things you need to keep in mind is how you grow wealth without paying excess tax – and maybe, even better, significantly improving your tax position as you go along. You might think that sounds kind of crazy but let me assure you that you are taxed the most on what you earn. There are a number of ways you can save tax by considering what your money earns for you. A lot of the ways in which your money earns for you can be very tax efficient. So, another great reason to build wealth is that it is taxed significantly more generously than how your income is taxed.

MAKING YOUR MONEY WORK FOR YOU

One way you can make your money work for you is by being paid dividends from Australian companies. This type of income will usually come with franking credits. What is so great about franking credits is that they are actually counted as prepaid tax. Usually with fully franked income that means you are getting a 30% credit on that income. That is pretty awesome.

Another way that you can make your wealth work for you is through property trusts and their ability to provide tax-deferred income. This works like depreciation on a property you buy direct. Imagine you were to receive $10,000 income. Of that income, $8,000 might be tax deferred, meaning you only pay tax on the remaining

$2,000. With this, though, the tax-deferred amount increases your capital gains (or decreases your capital loss) by that amount. Of course, in Australia capital gains are reduced by 50% then taxed so it is still a really great outcome: you defer when you pay tax and then on that deferral you are likely to only pay half, or maybe even less if the tax rates reduce!

USING DEBT TO YOUR ADVANTAGE

Now, I can't keep talking about increasing your money with tax advantages without talking about debt and how you can use it to your advantage. In chapter 4 I talked about good debt versus bad debt in detail, so go back and read the chapter again if you are still not convinced that consumer debt is the devil.

As I said in chapter 4, good debt is debt that helps you improve your cashflow. It is usually debt that also allows you to claim the interest as a tax deduction. Because of this, using debt as part of your strategy to build wealth and increase your cashflow can work to your advantage. However, you still have to be careful about the amount of debt you take on. The purpose of using debt is to help improve your after-tax cashflow from investing. Ideally any investment that you make should be able to pay for itself. An investment shouldn't require ongoing contributions – if it does, it isn't an asset but a liability. Yes, I am saying that whatever you are investing in should be standing on its own, unless it has another specific purpose. Alternatively, if it can be funded by other investments you have that is also okay. This approach helps you build sustainable cashflow so that you are able to enjoy financial freedom. Remember, I am talking about increasing the money in your buckets, so you don't want to invest in something that takes money from your buckets!

Debt can help or hinder. If it's managed well and you don't accrue too much of it, it can be a great way to increase your returns and make a large difference to your financial position. However, too much of it will trap your cashflow and you will be spending your funds paying your debt down or paying interest, rather than increasing the money in your buckets.

A great example of how you can use debt to help with cashflow is to use a margin loan to help you buy some growth investments. Doing this will allow you to invest more money, getting more skin in the game. If you invest in the current market you will receive approximately 4.2% net dividend with another 1.5% tax credit (total 5.7%), and you can get a margin loan at 4%. By investing 50% from a margin loan (on a total investment of $500,000), in one year you will pay $10,000 in interest, and receive $21,000 in dividends and $7,500 in tax credits. At the marginal tax bracket of 34.5% (the most common) you will net $12,117.50 in your first year. Also remember the cost to buy the investment in this strategy might be 0.25%. This is just an example, and as previously mentioned diversification is key so it can be a good idea to make ongoing contributions over time, so you can build your portfolio. Now as time goes on the use of leverage will improve your net return. More importantly though doing this does not decimate your cash returns.

For comparison's sake, let's say you buy an investment property and pay $1 million for the property plus $50,000 in costs. Now, from that investment you are likely to receive rent of $750 per week. If you borrow 80% for the purchase of this property, you will receive net rent of approximately $27,300 per annum when you allow for repairs and maintenance. You will pay interest of $28,000 at 3.5%. On top of that you will still have to make principal repayments on the loan. Repayments are likely to be $3,600 a month. Even with tax deductions at 39% you are looking at net cashflow of -$13,400 per annum. You are completely reliant on capital growth to get a return on your investment. Remember that you also contributed $250,000 to this investment. That is a $25,517.50 differential in cashflow per annum. Also, I was being generous with net rental return as typically over the long term landlords get to keep approximately one third of their rent – yes, only 33%. So, in this example over the long term you may only net $13,000 of the total $39,000 you receive.

Also remember that any positive cashflow that you are receiving from an investment can provide compounding returns as well. Even if you don't reinvest the full amount and split it equally across your buckets you will still have more cashflow in your buckets and be closer to the freedom that you want.

When you are using debt, you are essentially using other people's money to get investment outcomes. Now, I have spoken about using debt to help generate wealth in a balanced way. However, it is also possible to use other people's money to get access to markets without putting any capital at risk. People are creating products all the time that allow you to borrow 100% and get the returns of the market back in return. What you have to spend to get access to it depends on the product and its development. However, it is possible to get access to global markets (and even local markets) for approximately 5% per annum and net cost of as low as 1% per annum of what is invested. It is best to be getting advice when using products like this. While they can provide a lower-risk way of getting into the markets they are generally not a long-term investment and usually only run for three to five years, and are therefore subject to some of the other risks mentioned in chapter 7.

That said, using a product like this can work well for someone who is more conservative with their capital but still wants access to the growth of the capital markets. With a diversified defensive strategy, you can earn 4% per annum. Let's say you have $100,000. A three-year investment in one of these products might cost you $10,000 for the three years. That leaves you with $90,000. If you get 4% per annum at the end of the three years you will have $101,238 plus any growth you make in your market investment. If it doesn't perform you have still preserved your capital.

These types of investments can help get you great risk-adjusted returns but need to be part of a wider overall financial plan. Risk-adjusted returns just means the anticipated return based on the risk taken. Most people would have heard that you need to take on more risk to get more return. With some of these strategies you can get great risk-adjusted returns as the risk you are taking is not that great, but you can still get great returns.

THERE IS MOST VALUE WHEN THINGS SEEM BAD

As I am writing this book, we are about 15 years out from the global financial crisis (GFC). It started in mid 2007 and was in full swing by late 2008 when financial markets froze. The markets didn't plummet, they froze. Banks would not lend money to each other for fear they would not be there the next day. The global banking sector almost collapsed overnight. It was serious stuff. Even our good strong Aussie banks hit up our prime minister on a Friday and said if something wasn't done by Monday they would be insolvent. That is why we had an announcement guaranteeing bank debt and deposits on Sunday 12 October 2008. However, the GFC continued and markets remained in freefall.

In March 2009 most markets including the Australian market had reached the lowest point in the cycle. By September 2009 the market had increased almost 50%. The reason for me telling you this is that when things seem bad it's actually when there is the most value to be found. Good companies were still good companies even during the GFC. The opposite is also true. When everything is going really well there is the least amount of value to be found.

In bad times the worst thing you can do is run out and take your money. Imagine if you had taken your money out in March 2009 when the market was at its lowest? No, seriously, just imagine doing that. Imagine that you had a substantial amount of your money in the market. You panicked and took it out in March 2009. I remember speaking to a potential client who wanted to take all of his money out of the market in February 2009. I remember saying to him if that is all he wants he can go and speak to someone else. I personally doubled down and borrowed money and invested in the market shortly after the market had reached the bottom, and almost doubled what I had invested in six months. I am not suggesting you take the same risk, but I know my business and knew the market was somewhere near the bottom and I wasn't going to miss out.

When the news is telling you how good everything is it is usually already too late. But when it comes to investing in markets (regardless of the market) time and continuous investing are your best friends. If you had invested the day before the financial crisis in 1987 (just before I was born) you would still have had the best returns of all asset classes. Again, this is not a recommendation to invest just before a crash, but an example of how investing in business that creates value over time will give you great returns.

USING CONTRACTS

Another way that you can look to increase the money in your buckets and make some wealth is via contracts. By using contracts you can actually create wealth from almost nothing. What do I mean by this? Let's look at an example of when I personally did this. I found a commercial property, I refitted it out and put a lease on it. By putting a lease on the property I added 20% to its value. In other words, by putting a contract on the property I added 20% value. This is because commercial property is mostly valued based on the lease that is in place on the property. Other factors do contribute to the value, but a strong lease will add the most value. So, all I had to do was add a contract (being a lease) to add significant value to the property.

There are whole professions that have been built around the use of contracts to add value, and to help people and businesses get the most value out of the markets as they are. You will see that a company will attempt to not issue debt and equity during market downturns but will always try to issue them at the height of the market. The reason for this is because they want to get money as cheaply as possible. This is why people work in building value and finding value in markets and contracts. They are looking at arbitraging what they see in the markets that they are operating – whether that be adding value to a property through a spruce up and new lease or taking advantage of market conditions for a company's benefit.

USING TAX CODE – RECYCLING DEBT

Another way to improve your cash position is to recycle your debt and use the tax code within Australia to your advantage. If you are not currently investing, one of the best things you can do with your spare cash is to put the excess against an offset account on your home mortgage – or, if your mortgage has redraw available (most do), put it directly against the mortgage. This will save you interest on your loan.

In Australia you are taxed on interest you earn but not on interest you save, so if you can save interest by putting money against your home loan or in a mortgage offset this gives you a saving on the interest on your home loan, which you don't have to pay any tax on. Now that is a pretty good return.

However, something that can work even better is to recycle your debt. This is the process of turning your debt from non-tax-deductible to tax-deductible debt. You can do this by splitting out your loan into two parts, or even changing how you redraw from your home loan. Your aim is to redraw from your home equity or home loan to invest. This redraw is then tax deductible. Then, instead of paying down the investment part of the loan, you want to put the extra income and all of your repayments towards the non-tax-deductible part of your loan. If you don't split your loan this can still work well. If you have a regular home loan and have redraw available, what you can do is only redraw from your home loan for investment purposes; as you consistently redraw from your home loan you will increase the tax-deductible portion of your loan. Over time that means that you will have only tax-deductible debt and no non-tax-deductible debt.

This recycling of debt helps you with your cashflow as you will decrease the amount of tax you pay and if invested properly you will build a passive cashflow.

USING SUPER TO INCREASE CASHFLOW

Something else that you can do is invest money into your super-annuation and get a return back personally. To do this you need to have a self-managed superannuation fund (SMSF). This allows you to lend money to your super fund for investing. If you lend money to your super fund for investing in equities (the share-market) you are able to lend up to 50% of the value over a term of seven years. What is great about this strategy is the interest rate for lending money to yourself is currently 7.1% – compare this to the 1% you will get from the banks. This is a great return. There are also advantages in that the interest is tax deductible and can offset tax payable on your contributions; and if invested properly the credits from your investments will substantially reduce your contributions tax. It can even be possible to work it so that your fund isn't paying any contributions tax on the money. Remember, while you are doing this you are getting a 7.1% interest rate on your money.

BECOMING A SOPHISTICATED INVESTOR

As you build your wealth you will want to build enough wealth or have enough income to be classed as a sophisticated investor. Not being classed as a sophisticated investor isn't going to stop you being successful in building your wealth, but being classed as one opens up many more investment doors. When you are classed as a sophisticated investor you get first dibs on investment opportunities and you will also have many more investment opportunities open to you (a lot of investments are only available to sophisticated investors).

The point of putting these strategies into play is to use the system and your investments to help increase what's in your money buckets. When you start using everything available to you in tandem you will see a substantial improvement in your cashflow – even if you don't increase your income from working at all. It is important that you use this increased cashflow in proportion in your buckets and then you will get the benefits of further compound interest on your returns.

ACTION POINTS

- Get your money working for you.

- Consider how to use debt to your advantage. Debt recycling anyone?

- Consider opportunities to use contracts to increase value.

- Use your superannuation to boost your wealth in more than one way.

- Work towards becoming a sophisticated investor.

CHAPTER 9

WHAT TO DO WITH YOUR FREEDOM

The purpose of everything that I have set out in this book is for you to be a boss and live the life you want to live. Everyone has a different version of what this looks like but it is important that you actually take the time to enjoy it along the way. At the end of the day it is not just the destination that is important but also the journey in getting there. To me being a boss and living life is nothing more than doing what I want when I want.

In this chapter I will explore how you can enjoy the journey on the way while ensuring that you meet your goals as well. Then I will look at what is important and ways you can manage your energy to get the most out of yourself.

First, let's explore the importance of money.

MONEY ENABLES LIFE

Money by itself is meaningless but it is a highly important enabler if you want to do the things you want in life. If you want to help your kids buy their first car or even their first house you need money. If you want to help people in extreme poverty you need money to help further your cause. Whatever it is you are looking at doing, it will require money. It might not necessarily be *your* money, but all these things require funding from somewhere.

So, don't let people tell you money isn't important. It is vitally important to function in society and it is crucial in helping you get what you want. People who think money isn't important tell themselves that because they don't have any, nor will they. However, let me be clear on something: money is not *the* most important thing – far from it – but it is important.

MANAGING YOUR ENERGY

Now that we have established that money does have a big impact on your ability to do the things that you want, let's explore how to get the most out of your time and money so that you can enjoy living life while getting on track to having what you want. You must remember that the only finite resources you have are your available energy and time. So, you must be very purposeful with how you use them! As it is the only finite resources you have they are also the most valuable. You will see that I have included the term 'energy' along with 'time'. Personally, I believe energy is what you have to manage more than time. Depending on what you are doing you will only have so much energy until you run out on that task. Everyone is different when it comes to this. Think of it like running. Some people can run a marathon with energy to spare. Other people can only run two kilometres. We all have different capabilities, so it's vitally important that we manage our energy to get the most out of our capabilities. Maybe we shouldn't be running if we can only go two kilometres, but we might be able to do a five kilometre swim!

I highly recommend reading Tim Ferriss's excellent book *The 4-Hour Work Week*. Much of what he talks about in his book is even more relevant today than when he first wrote it. The key thing that I got out of this book was to eliminate distraction to free up time. Focus on the 20% that is important. This is more essential than ever as we are constantly distracted by email, instant chat (Teams, Slack), social media and a constant barrage of news from any and all sources.

Another important way you can start managing your energy is making sure that you get the most out of meetings. Most meetings take about 10 times longer then they need to. One way I have managed to get around this is by having stand-up meetings with a very strict agenda. Having stand-up meetings means that people don't want to hang around any longer then they need to, and having a strict agenda means that the meeting stays on track. All meetings should have a purpose, an outcome and action points for those who attended. If you're not in a position to change how meetings are run I suggest giving your ideas to your superiors. Alternatively, start being much more selective with the meetings you attend. Remember: it is your time and life so you need to take control where you can. You will probably find that you are able to get a lot more real work done rather then sitting in on meetings you weren't really required for.

Next, consider how you start the day. Do you begin by looking at your email, or the notifications on your smartphone? If you do, then you are most likely not getting the most out of your day. When you start your day off like this you are giving yourself over to other people's agendas. Instead, consider the SAVERS method detailed in Hal Elrod's book *The Miracle Morning*. SAVERS stands for:

- **S**ilence – gives you time to reflect
- **A**ffirmations – allows you to start positively
- **V**isualisation – allows you to see what you want
- **E**xercise – makes you the best you; makes you feel better
- **R**eading – something inspiring drives creativity and productivity
- **S**cribing – allows you to plan out your day and put in the things you are grateful for.

All of these are important to do. They will give you the absolute best start to your day and allow you to fulfil your potential.

My last piece of advice to manage your energy is to get rid of negative time-wasters from your life. You know who these people are. All they seem to do is complain about things in the world and think that the world owes them everything, but they aren't really willing to do anything to get it themselves. Remove them from your life as they are toxic and will not help you in any way, shape or form. Remember: you are the average of the five people that you hang around with.

Now it is time to start putting all your plans into place. Calendar planning is something that is absolutely vital. But what the hell is it?

Calendar planning is where you book in everything that you want to do. I mean everything. You book in time for your kids, you book in time for your partner, you book in time for personal and professional development. Put it all in there. Don't leave anything out. By planning it and putting it in the calendar your goals become appointments that you aren't going to miss.

Calendar planning works alongside routine, and routine allows you to be free. If you have a routine you do not need to think as much about what you are going to do. So, my suggestion is to also build routine into some of the activities that you put in your calendar. For instance, you might decide that you would like to spend one hour per week with each of your children to do something just with each other, without anyone else in the family. If you book that in your calendar you then have an appointment, and if you do it at the same time each week both you and your child know when to expect it.

I suggest having an electronic calendar. They are absolutely awesome and make your life so much better due to the way they enable you to invite other people to your appointments and receive auto reminders via email, SMS and phone notifications. I also suggest that you have a physical calendar in addition to the electronic version. The physical calendar might not be set up as a traditional calendar. In our family we have a physical calendar that is split into different sections for different things that we are doing. A quick glance at this calendar means that I know (and everyone else in the family knows) what events we are attending, what getaways we have planned and what meeting my wife and I might have on after hours.

If possible, it's a good idea to colour code your calendar so that you know which different events are on at a quick glance. The categories I suggest are:

- Work – anything that relates to work
- Family – anything that relates to the whole family
- Kids only – anything that relates to the kids
- Partner only – anything with your partner
- You only – anything that is for yourself.

If you are running separate work and personal calendars I suggest marking on your personal calendar when you are at work, and marking on your work calendar when you are not at work.

It is also important to book out time for holidays. The advantage of this type of planning is that you end up booking holidays anywhere up to 18 months in advance, so you have heaps of room to move within your calendar. I personally don't like to book anything more than a couple of days with less than six months' notice. Also book in time for short getaways. I personally love getaways – getting away for a couple of days is a great way to recharge and it is amazing where you can go and what you can do with a few days. With getaways and vacations my suggestion is to book in the time to go away and then work out what you are going to do later if you are not sure now. If you book in the time you at least know that you are going to go away somewhere.

Let's now talk about the importance of putting aside time for the most important person in your life. That person is you. If you do not put time for yourself in your calendar and do not look after yourself first you will not be able to look after others.

It is pretty simple. You need to look after a few areas in your life and make sure you put yourself first so you are the best you. The areas I suggest are:

- Physical health
- Mental health
- Money
- Spirituality.

Let's take a look at each of these.

Physical health

If you end up fat and unfit you will have less energy than someone who is fit and healthy. If you have less energy, you are going to be able to give less of yourself to your family. If you are not in a good state, you are also more likely to die sooner meaning that you don't even get to spend as many years with the people you claim you care most about. So, it is important that you look after yourself physically.

Mental health

It is really important to stay super sharp and focused mentally in this day and age – and this is becoming harder to do! With all the distractions that we have around us it can be really tricky to let your mind have a break, but it is so vitally important to do so. I think managing your energy and your mental health is one of the most important things you can do. If you are not right in your head how do you think you will be able to help others? I am not saying that you can't help others if you suffer from a mental health condition; I mean that you need to be on top of it and managing it to be able to help others. I personally keep a journal as a tool to maintain my mental health. It is about getting the most out of yourself – not necessarily about fixing problems. Keeping yourself in top shape mentally will make you a lot more creative and productive and put you in good stead to give your best to everything that you do.

Money

What do I mean by putting your money needs first? I am talking about paying yourself first, which I have mentioned before. It is important that you put your financial needs first so that you are able to build the lifestyle that you require. There's no point putting everyone else's needs first and finding that you all of sudden have a lot of personal debt and are struggling to pay for it all. It is important that you don't put yourself in a position where you are struggling financially to meet others' needs. People need to respect you and what you are after as well!

Spirituality

Okay, this might sound a bit fluffy and I suppose it kind of is. This isn't about getting in touch with God or anything like that. To be spiritual is separate from being religious. What I am talking about is being happy with who you are right now and the circumstances that you are in. That doesn't mean you don't want to improve your circumstances regardless of what they are, but you are happy with you as you are right now regardless. I think the best way to be happy with yourself is to know that you are doing your best to improve yourself in all areas. When you are doing that, regardless of your circumstances at that point in time, you can take the time to appreciate what you have and who you are giving the best of you to. This is something that I believe cannot come from external factors, but you have to find for yourself. If you are happy with yourself knowing that you are being the best that you can be at the given time, then you will find yourself in a much better state of mind and in a place where you are able to give your all to others. Why? Because you know that you are doing your best and are being the best you can be right now!

ENJOYING LIFE ALONG THE WAY

Now, you might be wondering how you can possibly manage all this, plus spend time with your family, take time away and do the things you want. How do you actually get to the part of saving money and creating the funds to live the lifestyle that you want to?

First, there is the impact of professional advice and how much of a difference that can make in terms of how much 'extra' you have to play with. There is also the fact that you do not need as much as you probably think you do. You do not have to be travelling first class everywhere (or if you do, get the most out of your reward points). You can do things more cheaply than you think you can, and they can just be as enjoyable – maybe even more so. It really depends how you want to do things.

It is important though to make sure that you don't hold off on doing things that you enjoy – that you still make time to go away for trips and enjoy living life. The truth is that you don't really know how long you will be here for, so you need to make the most of life while you can enjoy it.

Here are some ideas on how you can find ways to enjoy life a bit more along the way.

Find a hobby

Find a hobby you enjoy and make time for it. It is best to make sure you book time in your calendar and make room in your budget for it. If you do that you will be able to really enjoy it.

Go on mini holidays

Go away for a weekend or a few days. Not only is this enjoyable, you will find that you can go away a lot more often if you do this.

Personally I love camping and caravans. They make it cheap and you can almost go anywhere.

Look locally for tourist attractions

It might amaze you to find out about the entertainment and tourist attractions available in your local area. People often forget to look locally at what they can do. This can be a great way to get out for the day or even the weekend for one of those mini holidays I mentioned.

Start small

If you have something big and expensive that you want to do, start by thinking smaller and investigating cheaper ways that you might be able to do that activity. You can almost do anything on a smaller budget – you just have to be smart and look for opportunities.

For instance, you might be wanting to go boating and considering buying a boat. Maybe you have someone that you can share the cost with, so that the cost of boating is cheaper for both of you.

Or you might want to get into car racing or drags. Again, it might be better to share the experience with someone else so that you can work together and get more enjoyment out of the experience.

Don't forget that there are always going to be other people who want to do what you want to do, and you could possibly share the experience and even the costs with them. Doing these things with others who also have the same passion can result in having a more enjoyable experience. Not only that, when you pool resources you might be able to do more than you could have done yourself!

Other options

Finally, and this idea is a bit 'out there', but have you ever considered being a full-time wanderer? 'What the hell do you mean by that?' I hear you ask.

Becoming a wanderer means not having a fixed address and travelling full time. It doesn't mean you are in the car driving every day – you might stay in one location for a few weeks before you move on. If seeing the world is big on your list of things to do, you can consider this. The cost of being a wanderer can be cheaper than being in a fixed location. What?! How? When you are in a fixed location you have a lot of costs associated with being in that location – whether it be rent, mortgage repayments, utilities and the list goes on. If you get yourself a good caravan you will just have to pay some site fees as you travel, which you will find are probably similar to the amount of rent that you pay for a place in the city. A city apartment might cost $800 a week to rent, which is around $114.29 per day – and that's not including other costs.

It's a bit of a tangent but something to think about if you are interested.

BUILDING FLEXIBILITY INTO YOUR WORK

Whether you're working in your own business or for an employer, it is vital to have the freedom to live the way that you want by building flexibility into your work. Flexibility is a priority for me, so I have built significant flexibility into the work I do. Most days, I am home by the time my children have come home from school. I am able to help with all of their extra activities, as well as make sure dinner is made and so on. Not only that, I am at home in the mornings, too, to ensure the kids get off to school.

If you are in your own business and wondering how you go about this, it is pretty simple: business by design, not default. It is your business, so you can make your own rules and set the parameters that you work by. You take full responsibility for the business you have. If you don't like what you have created, change it! Remember, you are your own boss, so be a boss.

As a result of the flexibility that I created within my business I was able to look after my two sons while my wife and stepdaughter went over to the US for a trip with my mother-in-law. I could do that because I built enough flexibility in my business to allow me to manage my work wherever I have an internet connection and my phone or laptop.

If you aren't in charge and are working for someone else, speak to them about giving you flexibility to work from home or have a hybrid working arrangement. I think any self-respecting employer should be creating flexibility to attract and hold on to the best people out there. Anyone who respects the value you can and do bring will allow you that flexibility.

Building this sort of flexibility into your work and doing something that you really enjoy makes work feel like it's not work at all. It makes it more like having a hobby that you get paid for. If you can do that, I think you can say that you have created a significant amount of freedom for yourself.

ACTION POINTS

- Rethink meetings. Can you do them better?

- Consider how you start your day. Consider trying out the SAVERS ritual.

- Start calendar planning. Book everything in!

- Look after yourself first – make sure time for yourself is booked in.

- Find out what you want to do and plan for time to live life.

- Build flexibility into your work.

PUTTING IT ALL TOGETHER

Congratulations! You have made it to the end of the book. This small final chapter gives you a quick summary of the key learnings of this book so that you are able to put it all together.

The first thing that you will need to work on before you can build any significant wealth is your mindset on money. You need to be conscious of self-sabotage and work on your story when it comes to money. Money is unlimited and infinite – you just need to get your part of the pie, and you deserve it!

Now, what are your goals? Have you written them down? Is someone going to keep you accountable? You now know that someone who writes their goals down and commits to someone else to achieve them has a much greater chance of achieving their goals. Be purposeful and make your goals a reality!

Next, work on your understanding of assets and liabilities. What do your assets and liabilities look like? How is your cashflow statement? Remember, the key to creating freedom is building cashflow to support you and what you are after.

Now, what is your debt like? Understand your debt situation and the different types of debt. Don't be afraid to use debt in a positive way – it can be your ally in building a sustainable cashflow stream. It is also important that you get the right professional help to guide you the right way.

Now it is time for you to understand what your money buckets look like. How can you improve the way you are allocating funds to your money buckets? Next, you need to work out a budget that you can work within. Remember to compare your budget to your actual spending. Keep improving your budget and make sure you live life while putting money into the wealth bucket.

Next, consider how to build diverse cashflow. If you are like most people you will have no diversity in your cashflow. Remember, every dollar earned from other sources helps you diversify away from one income stream. When you are investing your funds it is important to make sure diversity is considered. And don't forget to think outside the box for the generation of other income.

It is important to increase the amount in your buckets over time. You will be able to do this as you build your wealth, but it is also important to look at using the system that we work and live in to get advantages to make your buckets grow. Look at using contracts, the tax code and other people's money to help build your buckets.

An important final consideration is how to get the most out of your life. What are you wanting to do that you aren't? Consider doing things differently. You don't have to own things outright to get value and use out of them. Make some decisions now to get what you want out of life.

Now and go create the freedom you want. Be a boss with your money. It is up to *you* and *you* deserve it!

REFERENCES

Clarissa Bye and Chris Harris (2017), 'ABS household expenditure survey shows Australians spending more on restaurants and takeaway', *The Daily Telegraph*, dailytelegraph.com.au/news/nsw/abs-household-expenditure-survey-shows-australians-spending-more-on-restaurants-and-takeaway/news-story/5d71d67f8239e34 42906f9431fd5dbca.

Hal Elrod (2016), *The Miracle Morning: The 6 Habits That Will Transform Your Life Before 8AM*, John Murray.

MLC (2020), *MLC Wealth Submission: Retirement Income Review*, treasury.gov.au/sites/default/files/2020-02/mlc040220.pdf.

Robert T Kiyosaki (1997), *Rich Dad Poor Dad: What the Rich Teach Their Kids About Money That the Poor and Middle Class Do Not!* Plata Publishing.

Stephen Newland (2018), 'The Power of Accountability', Association for Financial Counseling & Planning Education, afcpe.org/news-and-publications/the-standard/2018-3/the-power-of-accountability.

Tim Ferriss (2011), *The 4-Hour Work Week: Escape the 9-5, Live Anywhere and Join the New Rich*, Vermilion.

ABOUT THE AUTHOR

Peter started in the finance industry at the age of 17. By the age of 19 he was a fully licensed financial adviser and started his first business venture. At 21 Peter become a fully qualified accountant.

Peter went on to complete a Master of Commerce and started in partnership with accounting firm Preston Coe & Ring. Over time this business become PCR Accounting & Advisory, which Peter now leads.

Over the years Peter has become involved in a number of different businesses and has expanded his qualifications to become a specialist in succession, asset protection and estate planning.

Peter is not a typical accountant, having a background in finance and being in business for almost all of his entire adult life. He loves business because it is exciting, challenging and extremely rewarding. He loves helping those who get into business live life and thrive; he believes that owning a business can be an ideal way to build freedom and success.

Outside of work and business Peter loves to spend time with his kids and his wife. They enjoy everything to do with cars. A rewarding and exciting day for Peter involves getting up early in the morning to get a kickstart on the day; working hard to help his clients succeed; before leaving work in the afternoon (most days) to help with the kids' sports and home life.